THE VERY BEST PLACE FOR A PENNY

Written By
Dina Herman Rosenfeld

Illustrated By
Leonid Pinchevsky
Eliyahu Meshchaninov

© Copyright 1984
Second printing 1986

Merkos L'inyonei Chinuch, Inc.
770 Eastern Parkway
Brooklyn, New York 11213
(718) 774-4000 / 493-9250

Library of Congress Cataloging-in-Publication Data

Rosenfeld, Dina Herman.
    The very best place for a penny.

    Summary: Emphasizes the mitzvah or Jewish commandment of giving
charity, through the tale of a penny in a drawer contemplating the very best
place for himself.
    1. Charity--Juvenile literature. 2. Ethics, Jewish--Juvenile
literature. [1. Charity. 2. Commandments (Judaism)] I. Pinchevsky,
Leonid, ill. II. Meshchaninov, Eliyahu, ill. III. Title.
BJ1286.C5R67   1986   296.3'85   84-80764
ISBN 0-8266-0362-9
Printed in the United States of America

Merkos L'inyonei Chinuch, Inc.
New York

Once upon a time, there was a little, shiny penny.

He lived in a drawer with pens, pencils and keys.

The penny was glad he was not alone, but, he thought to himself,

"A drawer is *not* the best place for a penny!"

One day, the penny felt himself being taken out and put into a boy's pocket. It was very dark and crowded inside the pocket.

"Watch out!" called a paper clip, "here comes something else!"

"It's a penny," spoke up a ball of string, "just what we need!"

"You know," said a rubber eraser, "I can hardly breathe in here!"

The little penny was very uncomfortable in the bulging pocket.

"A pocket," he thought, "is *not* the best place for a penny!"

He was very excited when that evening, the little boy began to empty his pocket. Out went the paper clip, out went the ball of string, and out went the eraser.

"Now it's my turn," thought the penny. But instead of taking out the penny, the boy put on his pajamas and threw his pants into a corner.

"Wait!" cried the little penny, "please wait! You forgot me!" But the little boy did not hear him, and the penny spent a long night in the corner all by himself.

"A corner," he thought, "is *not* the best place for a penny!"

The next day, the little penny felt himself being taken down the stairs to the laundry room. Then he was put into the washing machine full of hot, sudsy water.

Swish, swish, went the washing machine. All the clothes got wet and soapy. So did the little penny.

"A washing machine," he thought, "is *not* the best place for a penny!"

Then, into the dryer went all the wet clothes.
Spin, spin went the dryer. How nice and warm it was inside! But how dizzy all the spinning made the little penny feel!

"A dryer," he thought, "is *not* the best place for a penny!"

Soon all the clothes were dumped into the laundry basket, and the little penny was with them.

Strong arms lifted the basket and back to the bedroom they went.

When the basket full of clothes was put down with a thump, out rolled the penny!

He rolled and rolled, across the room, faster and faster, until he found himself right under the bed.

It was very dusty under the bed, and much too dark for the little penny.

"Under a bed," he thought, "is *not* the best place for a penny!"

The little penny was so tired from all of his adventures, that he fell fast asleep. While the penny was sleeping, the little boy came into his bedroom bouncing a rubber ball. He threw it and caught it each time. But suddenly, the ball slipped through his fingers, rolled across the room, under the bed, bumped right into the penny, and woke him up!

"How did you get here?" asked the ball.

"It's a long story," answered the penny.

"First, I was in a drawer, then in a pocket, then in a corner, then in a washing machine, then in a dryer, and now under a bed. I wish I could find a place where I really belonged."

"Do you think the boy will find us under this bed?" asked the penny.

"Oh yes!" said the ball, "this happens to me all the time. I'm always rolling away, but he always finds me."

Sure enough, just then, the little boy stretched his hand out under the bed to find his ball.

"Here's my ball . . .! No, it's not. It's smooth, and flat, and just about the size of — —

A Penny! I found my penny and my ball, too!"

"Well, little penny," said the boy, "I know the very best place for you!"

The boy ran downstairs with the penny in his hand, past the ball, past the bed, over the basket, past the dryer and around the washing machine, until he reached the Tzedakah box on the window sill.

"There you go, little penny," he said, and dropped it through the slot!

The little penny was very glad to be in the Tzedakah box, because he had many friends there, dollars, quarters, nickels and dimes. But most of all, the little penny was glad to be used for a Mitz-vah.

"A Tzedakah box," he thought, "is really the *very* best place for a penny!"

Glossary

Mitzvah: good deed. One of the 613 commandments in the Torah.

Tzedakah: charity

OTHER TITLES IN THE

MERKOS YOUNG READERS' LIBRARY

Temple Israel

Minneapolis, Minnesota

IN MEMORY OF
CLAIR WOLFSON
BY
ROSE SCHLEIFF